Asher the Disaster

BY KIMBERLY SEXTON

For Asher, a **brother born**
to help in time **of** need.
For my s**tudent**s, may **your** light
al**way**s s**hin**e bright.

ISBN: 979-8-218-69546-0

The art for this book was created with watercolor pencils and permanent marker on watercolor paper.

Asher the Disaster

by Kimberly Sexton

From terrible stenches to paint catasrophes,

Asher's stories unfold when his mommy returns to work after maternity leave. Her inquisitive students find laughter in Asher's disasters, which soon helps soften Mom's angry heart to his mischievous deeds. Thanks to her students opening her eyes, she can now see past the chaos, the rooms with debris, and see the world as her students see.

Starting Up

- Enjoy reading the book with your child and open your mind to curiosities and discoveries.
- Read the title and wonder aloud what kind of disasters Asher will make.

After the Story

Ask your child questions about the story.
- What were your favorite messes Asher created?
- What are creations you like to make?

Reflect
- In your life messes, try to extend grace and forgive each others mistakes.

This is no ordinary kid story,
Nor one filled with fame, fortune, and glory.
But one with wet messes oh so severe,
and a little boy who likes to disappear,
to places of adventure all on his own
which tend to make Mommy and Daddy moan.

Asher the disaster first came to be,
with tales from Mommy after maternity leave.

Her students would ask, "What's Asher up to?"
In which she'd reply, "Here, let me tell you."

Asher's first story was
quite an ordeal.
He heard the fridge open
and raced for a meal!

Tip-tap, tip-tap, his quiet feet did scutter,
across the floor, one foot after another.
He climbed on up and reached high for the butter,
a bad mess of all things and oh the clutter!
As the food came crashing down, she sputtered,
"Asher! No, Asher! Now, listen to your mother!"

Very soon Mom became the most grinchiest grouch,
because he dumped cereal on top of the couch!

A whole box of Lucky Charms piled in a heap,
so tall, and so wide, and so high, and so steep!
One by one, Asher picked the marshmallows in sight,
and gladly ate them with delicious delight.

With wide smiles her students cried out,
"Tell us more!"
She said, "This mess was found on the
kitchen's wood floor!"

The fun started when Mommy heard giggles galore.
So, she decided to look instead of ignore
the splishing and splashing in puddles he poured,
from bottles of water onto the floorboards.

Just to make matters worse, on Christmas Eve,
Mom found Asher hiding behind the bright tree
and discovered a scent which was smelly indeed.
Before she knew it, her nose started to twitch,
due to his diaper's most terrible stench.

So, she quickly rushed Asher inside his bedroom,
With a zip, with a zap, and a zing, and a zoom –
to dispose of the stinky and foul-smelling fumes.

Then, as the clock struck two in the dead of night,
"BANG, BANG" boomed from Asher's room and caused a fright!
Frizzled and frazzled, Mom turned on the light,
and found Asher playing drums with all his might!
"What's next," you ask? She described the sweet sight.

All of Asher's choo choo trains were nestled in bed,
with books of dinosaurs and bears being read,
by a boy who would make up stories in his head,
for his mind grew wild with words to be said.

The kids loved the stickiest story by far,
and without a doubt, most totally bizarre!
Asher's Mom left him alone and came to find,
a new box of Oreos and crumbs left behind.

Turning the corner, she saw what she feared.
Every single Oreo, opened and smeared –
across the table and inside his small ears!
Mommy learned her lesson for the story shows,
she should never leave out a box of Oreos.

The next story happened while Mom folded clothes.
With a thump and a boom, a loud racket arose.
Mom ran quickly to check on the thunderous thud,
and found Asher painting inside the bathtub!

He still wore his clothes with a broad smile on his face,
using soap of all colors to spruce up the place.
But Mom turned on the water and didn't refrain,
from washing his big masterpiece down the drain.

And now, the messiest story of all.
Asher splattered paint on more than just walls!
From the art room window to the front door,
a trail of paint led to his bedroom floor.
On the tv stand, smearing his table and chairs,
paint covered his toys and colored his hair.
Asher used his hands to spread paint everywhere!

Mom's patience was up,
she couldn't take anymore,
"Off to bed you shall go!",
she said with a roar.

At long last, she plopped down, so woefully weary,
after cleaning his messes, so wet and smeary.
She took a deep breath and asked God in faith,
to increase her patience and allow room for grace.

Because her anger didn't do any good,
toward her playful son whom she misunderstood.

For when Asher made disasters, Mom knew by heart,
he was a special boy to be set apart.

From yelling and fussing, so he'll discover
the child inside, his own person to uncover.

One day, Asher would grow up and be an adult
and his many adventures would be the result,

of a mom who found laughter in the disasters,
since her students helped her see what really mattered.

Not messes, not chaos, nor rooms with debris,
but seeing the world as her students see.

By leaving room for discoveries, indeed,
they will grow into who they're truly meant to be.

So, to students here and kids from afar,
you must always stay true to who you are!
Always look up, beam with brilliance like the stars,
and let your light shine from the dreams in your heart.

www.ingramcontent.com/pod-product-compliance
Lightning Source LLC
Chambersburg PA
CBHW060836270326
41933CB00002B/103